Egyptian Pyramids

BY ELIZABETH RAUM

RiverStream

RiverStream
Great Reading • Real Learning

Amicus High Interest hardcover edition is an imprint of Amicus
P.O. Box 1329, Mankato, MN 56002
www.amicuspublishing.us

Copyright © 2015 Amicus. International copyright reserved in
all countries. No part of this book may be reproduced in any
form without written permission from the publisher.

RiverStream Publishing reprinted with permission of
Amicus Publishing.

Library of Congress Cataloging-in-Publication Data
Raum, Elizabeth, author.
 Egyptian pyramids / Elizabeth Raum.
    pages cm. – (Ancient wonders)
 Summary: "Describes the pyramids of ancient Egypt, one of
the ancient wonders of the world, including how and why they
were built, the pharaohs who were buried inside, and what the
ruins are like today"–Provided by publisher.
 ISBN 978-1-60753-466-2 (library binding) –
 ISBN 978-1-60753-681-9 (ebook)
 1. Pyramids–Egypt–Juvenile literature. 2. Egypt–Antiquities–
Juvenile literature. I. Title. II. Series: Ancient wonders.
 DT63.R38 2014
 932.01–dc23
                                    2013028241

Editors   Quinn Arnold and Rebecca Glaser
Series Designer   Kathleen Petelinsik
Book Designer   Heather Dreisbach
Photo Researcher   Kurtis Kinnemann

Photo Credits
Superstock, cover; Shutterstock, cover bkgd., iStockphoto,
5; Shutterstock, 6; Superstock, DeAgostini / SuperStock ,
9, 10; Dreamstime/Prillfoto, 13; Alamy/Stock Connection
Blue, 14; Alamy/GlowImages, 17; Science Photo Library/
Christian Jegou/Photo Researchers, Inc., 18; Superstock, cover,
20; Alamy/Andrew Holt, 23; Dreamstime, 25; DeAgostini/
SuperStock, 26; Getty Images/Will & Deni McIntyre, 29

1 2 3 4 5 CG 18 17 16 15 14
RiverStream Publishing–Corporate Graphics,
Mankato, MN–042014
ISBN 978-1-62243-239-4 (paperback)

Table of Contents

The Mysteries of the Pyramids

A pyramid towers over the sand in Egypt. This ancient wonder was built more than 4,600 years ago. It is the Great Pyramid of Giza. It's the biggest pyramid. But there are dozens more pyramids in Egypt. Who built them? Why? How? An **Egyptologist** is a scientist who studies the pyramids. The scientists try to answer all these mysteries.

The Great Pyramid is the tallest one. It's over 450 ft (137 m) high. That's as tall as a 42-story building.

Pharaoh Khafre was one of the great pyramid builders.

Q Were all Egypt's kings buried in pyramids?

The Pyramid Builders

Egypt was a rich **empire**. It was strong too.

A **pharaoh**, or king, ruled Egypt.

The people thought that he was a god.

They thought that he would join the other

gods in heaven when he died. A pyramid

was a **tomb**. The pharaoh was buried in it

when he died.

 No. Some pharaohs built pyramids.
Some built other kinds of tombs.

The Egyptians believed in many gods. But Atum was the most important god. He was the sun god. The people thought that he died at night when the sun set in the west. He came alive again when the sun came up. They put the pyramids on the west side of the Nile River. That way, when a pharaoh died, he could follow Atum to heaven.

Egyptians prayed to a god named Atum.

A pyramid complex had several buildings with a high wall around them.

 Q Why was there a high wall?

A pyramid isn't just a big triangle sitting alone. Workers made other buildings near it. They made a smaller pyramid for the queen. They made tombs for pharaoh's friends. They built a **temple** so that the people could pray to the gods. This group of buildings was called a **pyramid complex**. A high wall was built around it.

The pyramid had things the pharaoh might want in his next life. It held jewelry, gold, furniture, and even food. The wall was made to keep robbers out.

Building the Pyramids

Many people in ancient Egypt were farmers. They grew crops such as wheat and barley. For a few months each year, the Nile River flooded. Farmers could not work in the fields. That's when they built pyramids. When the flood was over, they went back to their farms.

The Nile River floods every year.

The Step Pyramid is the oldest pyramid in Egypt.

Q Why isn't the pyramid white now?

The Step Pyramid was the first pyramid in Egypt. Imhotep was a priest. He planned it for the pharaoh Djoser. Imhotep built a stone base. Then he added five big stone steps. He covered it all in white **limestone**. The white stone glowed in the sun. Djoser was buried in it.

Robbers took the white stone. They used it in other places.

The next pharaohs built pyramids, too. They had problems. Some pyramids fell apart. Some were never finished.

With practice, the Egyptians became good builders. They measured very carefully. Each pyramid began with a perfect square. It was built on a hard rock. It took 20,000 to 30,000 men to do the work.

 How did the Bent Pyramid get its name?

King Snefru had the
Bent Pyramid built.

 It was too steep. It began to cave in. So the builders made changes halfway to the top.

17

Ramps helped workers drag huge blocks of stone up to a pyramid.

Q How heavy are the big blocks?

Workers put a ramp next to the pyramid. They pulled the huge blocks up the ramp. The pyramid got taller. So did the ramp. It was hard, slow work. Workers put a pointed **capstone** on top. They covered it all with white stone.

Each block weighed about 2.5 tons (2.3 t). That's as much as 25 refrigerators!

A village was built near each pyramid. Some people stayed all year. Some only stayed during the flood. Egyptologists looked at the ruins. They found large bakeries. Bakers made hundreds of loaves of bread every day. The workers ate bread, lamb, and beef.

Pyramid workers lived in houses made of stone. The ruins give us clues to how they lived.

Grave Robbers!

After a pharaoh died, the pyramid was closed up. The door was blocked by big stones. They tried to keep robbers out. But the robbers found ways to get in. They reopened the closed doors. They dug a new hole. They took anything they could find.

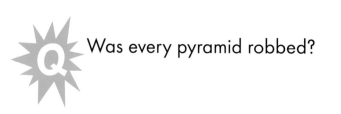 Was every pyramid robbed?

The large hole in this pyramid was made by grave robbers.

A Many Egyptologists think so.

Tourists came to see the pyramids too. The Greeks and Romans visited. Then people came from Europe and the Middle East. They took statues, pottery, and other riches home with them. A big stone from the Great Pyramid of Giza is now in London's British Museum. Many of Egypt's treasures are gone.

This obelisk from ancient Egypt was taken to Turkey.

A pyramid has several rooms inside. This is a burial chamber.

The Pyramids Today

Each year, about 4 million people visit the pyramids. They come from all over the world. Many come to see the Great Pyramid at Giza. A few lucky people are let inside it each day. They walk through the stone hallways. They see the pharaoh's tomb. People like to visit the pyramids. But today, the only thing they take is pictures.

Egyptologists used to think there were only 138 pyramids. But in 2011, a team of American Egyptologists found even more. They looked at **satellite** pictures. They saw 17 new pyramids. They were hidden in the sand. The Egyptologists will visit the sites. What will they find? What else is buried in the sand? We will have to wait and see.

Not all pyramids are as large as the Great Pyramid at Giza (below).

Glossary

capstone The stone at the very top of the pyramid.

Egyptologist A scientist who studies the pyramids and the life and culture of ancient Egypt.

empire A large territory joined under one ruler.

limestone A white rock used as a building material.

pharaoh A king or ruler of ancient Egypt.

pyramid complex A group of related buildings near a pyramid.

satellite A man-made object that circles Earth in space; some satellites take pictures of the surface.

temple A place to worship a god or gods.

tomb A place to bury a person's body after he or she dies.

Read More

Orr, Tamra. *Ancient Egypt*. Explore Ancient Worlds. Hockessin, Del.: Mitchell Lane Publishers, 2013.

Platt, Richard. *The Egyptians*. How They Made Things Work. Mankato, Minn.: Sea-to-Sea Publications, 2011.

Riggs, Kate. *Egyptian Pyramids*. Mankato, Minn.: Creative Education, 2009.

Websites

Egyptian Pyramids and Temples with Maps
http://www.eyelid.co.uk/pyr-temp.htm

NOVA Online/Pyramids: Scaling the Pyramids
http://www.pbs.org/wgbh/nova/pyramid/geometry/index.html

Pyramid Building Challenge
http://www.bbc.co.uk/history/interactive/games/pyramid_challenge/index_embed.shtml

Every effort has been made to ensure that these websites are appropriate for children. However, because of the nature of the Internet, it is impossible to guarantee that these sites will remain active indefinitely or that their contents will not be altered.

Index

About the Author

Elizabeth Raum has worked as a teacher, librarian, and writer. She has written dozens of books for young readers. She likes doing research and learning about new topics. After writing about ancient wonders, she wants to travel the world to visit them! To learn more, visit her website at www.elizabethraum.net.